Silence UTTERED

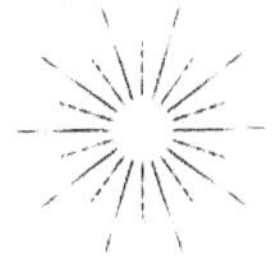

Also by Catherine Klinger

*Sacred Caregiving: Spiritual Solutions
for Providing End-of-Life Care*

Silence UTTERED

A Tale of Unity

Second Edition

CATHERINE KLINGER, Ph.D.

SECRETS-OF-LIFE
PUBLISHING

Silence Uttered

Second Edition

23005 N. 74th Street #2012
Scottsdale, AZ 85255
secretsoflifepub@gmail.com

ISBN: 978-0-9914835-5-6

Book design by Debbi Stocco

Library of Congress Control Number: 2014901827

Printed in the United States of America

Table of Contents

Prologue

alk into the forest
Come upon a brook
Listen to it babble
Like the verses in this book

Books and brooks are messengers
The Message has no name
Beyond all words and images
What's different is the same

The Beginning

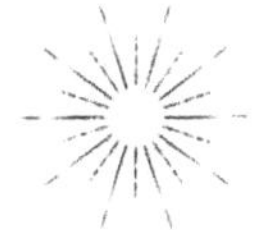

In the beginning
There were no words
No Rocks
No Trees
No Sky
No Birds

Nothing to see
Or be
Or do
No one to talk about
Or talk to

But Silence uttered

Silence uttered ONEness
That's all it had to say
Out of nowhere suddenly
ONE formless lump of clay

ONEness was not happy
ONEness was not sad
Life could not have been described
As either good or bad

Love did not exist of course
But neither then did hate
"I agree with me," sighed ONE
"There's nothing to debate"

"I'm here
I'm there
I'm everywhere
I'm everything," cried ONE
"It's not exactly boring, but
It's not exactly fun"

"I wonder what would happen if
I split myself in two
Variety could spice life up
And entertain me too"

"This change presents a problem
That really must be solved
Once the parts are separate
Why would they get involved?"

"I'll have to build the message in—
Design them with a clue—
Shape them so they'll interlock
They'll know just what to do"

Thus ONE began to chisel
To sculpt the perfect fit
Two jigsaw puzzle pieces
That could be merged or split. . .

The pieces started talking
They laughed and joked and played
ONEness was delighted with
The difference Twoness made

Twoness was delighted with
The thought of being ONE
"Me and You," said one of two
"Could have a lot of fun"

Silence uttered
Every time
Those jigsaw pieces
Merged
And that is how
The world was filled
With Rocks
And Trees
And Birds

The File Box

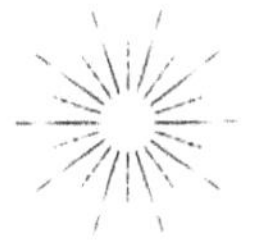

Rock sat down and sat and sat
Unmoved by this unmoved by that
Bird, in contrast, flew away
Sunrise lit the dawning Day

Rivers fed the Waterfall
Wind blew softly, Grass grew tall
Warm and pungent, lush and green
Calm, harmonious, pristine

Eventually, the discord came
Concocted by the human brain
A serpent by another name
Seeking fortune, seeking fame

Ego arrived to steal the wealth
Claiming the garden for himself
He frowned on Rock and Bird and Tree
"What good is all this Harmony?"

"These happy fools don't know what's wrong
That attitude won't last for long
Harmony is for the Birds
Egos have a need for Words"

"Words create duality
Objectify reality
Words cut up the Birds-eye view
Dividing me and we from you"

"A conqueror must first divide
Divisive Thoughts will be applied
When Differences are emphasized
They'll see the garden through my eyes"

"I'll segregate the Rocks from Trees
Make them think they're Enemies
To modify the Thoughts they think
I need the help of Pen and Ink"

"Let's build a box, a box of Words
Proper Nouns and 'To be' Verbs
Words that individualize
Stereotype and stigmatize"

"A File Box of Names and Places
Ages, Genders, severed Races
Everybody gets a niche
Poor can't mingle with the Rich"

"In The Box, there's a condition
'Live within your definition'
One file card per entity
Provides complete Identity"

"A card for Christian, one for Jew
Muslim, Buddhist, and Hindu
Separate cards for Sister, Brother
Pitting them against each other"

"The garden will be mine to seize
If I create some Hierarchies
Ranking them by Class and Caste
Guarantees some finish last"

"I'm always going to be the first
To quench my hunger and my thirst
I'll take it all and then take more
Exploiting's what an Ego's for"

"Greedy friends will hold top spots
Supervising the Have-nots
Sick? Weak? Homeless? Overpassed!
File the Desperate in the Trash"

"Once they know that Categories
Will determine their Life Stories
They'll succumb to Domination
Suffering Quiet Desperation"

"But Labeling is just the start
Of tearing garden roots apart
My monarchy will be complete
When I get subjects to compete"

"Watch and see me capitalize
While they are fighting for their lives
They're all boxed up; I've got their ear
To make them fight, I'll foster Fear"

"To foster Fear, I'll tell a lie:
Demand exceeds their scarce Supply
My ideal world Economy
Is based on Fear of Scarcity"

Ego declared a Reign of Greed
'Never Enough' conveyed his creed
His strategy could be defined
As 'Exploitative State of Mind'

Ego reigned and lines were crossed
Profit-making at any cost
Lives consumed by Acquisition
Fueled by vicious Competition

The Box was filled with Ego's rules
Lesson plans for all the schools
Exploitation caught on fast
Greed was popular at last

Keeping step with Ego's orders
Sets of nations with strong borders
Gathered up their hostile forces
Waging war for scarce resources

Killing those who can't be bought
Scorching Earth with battles fought
Not a drop was left to drink
Ego drove them to The Brink

Brinks are chinks in the flow of life
Openings that shed some Light
Fending off a grave attack
ONEness always has our back

At the Brink before the End
ONE engaged a trusted friend
Mirror made a fearless leap
Dropping into Ego's sleep

The Game

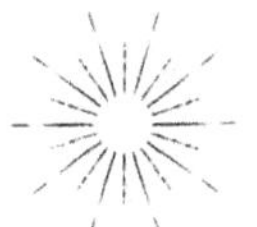

"Ego" said the Mirror
    "It's time to play The Game
    You'll see, despite appearances
    What's different is the same"

    "Give me your attention
    And I'll tell you what to do
    Take this ball and throw it out
    I'll throw it back to you"

Opponents took positions
One here—the other there
One served in, the other out
The ball flew through the air

In and out and out and in
From Me to You to Me
Mirror was a perfect match
They played whole-heartedly

Neither one could make a point
Love-Love the final score
"Can't we play some other game?
I'm good at tug-of-war"

"I want to win, to dominate
To conquer with my might
This game is lame and you're to blame
I'm ready for a fight"

Mirror answered mindfully
"If war is what you choose
You clearly think that winning means
Someone has to lose"

"Your File Box with its rusty Locks
Can be a dangerous toy
Need and Greed and Selfishness
Are costing you your Joy"

Ego heard a gasp for air
From somewhere deep within
The burden of his Selfishness
Was suffocating him

"My heart is detonating
With existential pain
I carved the world in pieces
For fortune and for fame"

"How can I end the suffering
If I am suffering too?
Mirror," Ego pleaded
"Please tell me what to do"

"Here's a way to play The Game
All by yourself instead
Of playing with opponents,"
The Mirror promptly said

"Place yourself both in and out
And in the middle too
Take the ball and throw it out
Then throw it back to you"

Dizzy with these twists and turns
An angry Ego said
"This game is so illogical
It's messing with my head!"

"What you're asking me to do
Simply can't be done
Can't you see I'll lose Myself?
This game cannot be won"

"You think too hard," said Mirror
"If thinking's all you do
You'll never find the joy in life
That lies in wait for you"

"It takes a choice, a leap of faith
To find joy in your heart
Be guided by your inner voice
Reflection is an art"

"Reflect," continued Mirror
"The Other Side is you
Shift yourself from here to there
By changing points of view"

"When you're looking out your eyes
The outside's what you see
Look in *and* out and live your life
With true Integrity"

Thus Ego looked inside and out
Looked ONEness in the eye
And—after much reflection—said
"I think You must be I"

The purpose of this insight
Was now quite plain to see
Ego took his journey
To find The Golden Key

"Empathy's The Golden Key
For a change in our direction
It frees us from the biases
That block our Reconnection"

"Before I saw Myself in You
I lived my life alone
The Game has turned me inside out
And paved my way back Home"

Revolution

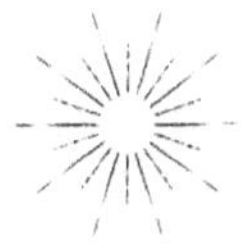

A turning point, a nexus
In the flow of evolution
Ego awoke and set the stage
For heart-felt Revolution

Revolving through the garden
He twirled The Golden Key
"I played a game that changed my mind
About Reality"

"Until I turned myself around
I wanted to be King
I boxed you up divisively
Polluting everything"

"The Golden Key of Empathy
Unlocks my Box of Lies
And liberates us from the Masks
That hide us in disguise"

"When I played The Mirror's Game
I got a chance to see
That who we always really are
Transcends Identity"

"Identity is foreground
Mere images we're seeing
Connectedness lies deep within
The essence of our being"

"Beyond the things we think we are
Beyond what we can name
Beyond all words and images
What's different is the same"

"We are different *and* the same
It's time to spread the word
On the outside, we are different
A Rock is not a Bird"

"Variety's the spice of life
What's different makes life fun
If only we'd remember
We started out as ONE"

"On the inside, we are Family
ONE constant common core
The Mission that unites us
Calls for The End of War"

"Join me in Revolution
My turnaround's a start
Everyone can make the shift
To living heart-to-heart"

The strength of their Compassion
Unfastened rusty Locks
Collectively, they overthrew
The old and musty Box

Chains of Thought fell to the ground
Forever bent and broken
Silence uttered in their hearts
When Words of Love were spoken

Flourishing as kindred souls
In jubilant rebirth
They saw themselves as gardeners
Sustainers of The Earth

Gratitude produced a stream
Of giving everywhere
Water flowed abundantly
To each an equal share

Sunshine filled the garden
With vital Energy
Fueling the beginning of
A new Economy

Scarcity ran out the gate
Once old rules were discarded
Fear ran too, along with Hate
"Let's get the party started"

"A party, yes, we'll throw a ball"
Said Bird to Rock and Tree
"Tonight's the night to celebrate
Divine Diversity"

Bird tweeted near and tweeted far:
TONIGHT COME ONE, COME ALL
RECONNECT, COME AS YOU ARE
COME TO THE PARTNERS BALL

Partners

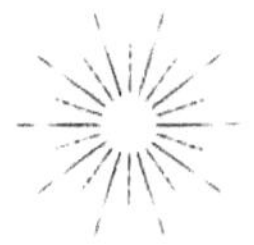

*I*t's Beginning now," said End
"Bring a Foe," insisted Friend
Out stepped In the ballroom door
Length chased Width across the floor

Fast relaxed and danced with Slow
Maybe danced with Yes and No
Dusk cut in on Day and Night
Gray cut in on Black and White

"Why be Average?" Low asked High
"Let's be Bold!" asserted Shy
"Let's be Happy," offered Sad
"Swing your partner, Good," said Bad

Networking throughout the night
"Nothing's Wrong," reported Right
"Nothing's missing," True told False
Partners joined in sultry waltz

Dinner bells began to chime

Fast and Slow got there on time

They all got there when they were able

Places for everyone at the table

Up sat Down, "It's time to eat"

Fat and Skinny shared a seat

Crazy settled next to Sane

"Fancy meal," requested Plain

"Don't be Sloppy," cautioned Neat
Bitter poured a drink for Sweet
All the Empty cups were Full
"There's a balance, Push" said Pull

"Add it up," advised Subtract
"Plus tells Minus how to act
It's a two-way interaction
Based on mutual attraction"

Simple smiled, "Life's Complex
She's Concave and He's Convex
Sometimes they're a perfect fit
Sometimes they can't wait to split"

"It's a puzzle, Lost then Found
"An enigma all around"
Silence laughed without a Sound
Superficial hugged Profound

"Take a Break," prescribed Repair
Hopefulness replaced Despair
Shallow dug down Deep inside
Narrow blossomed into Wide

Ordinary took the cue
"I'll be Special; you can too"
"I'll be Smoother now," said Rough
"I'll be Tender now," said Tough

"I'll be Quiet now," said Loud
"I'll be Humble now" said Proud
"I'll be Softer now," said Hard
"No one's Perfect," counseled Marred

"Thanks for shooting Straight," said Bent
"Things can Change," said Permanent
"Makes a Difference," Same replied
Lived agreed and quickly Died

Grieve shook hands with Celebrate
Early yawned, "It's getting Late"
Hot remarked, "It's getting Cold"
"Makes me tired, Young," said Old

Bottom looked around for Top
Off and On asked Start to Stop
To went From and Back went Forth
East drove West and South drove North

Right turned Left and Left turned Right
Dark turned off the ballroom Light
"Party's over Now," said Then
"Every night we'll dance again"

Epilogue

Deep asleep in dream tonight
As logic slips away
Find yourself remembering
The stillness of the clay

Make the reconnection
If you feel you are alone
In the still and silent space
All pathways lead to Home

Silence utters in our hearts
ONE simple Truth, unbroken
The Source remains Unthinkable
It's Whole and can't be spoken

Amazing people participated in the creation, design, and production of *Silence Uttered: A Tale of Unity.*

Zach English edited. Friends and colleagues offered support and recommended changes. In alphabetical order by first name, they included: Eva Hausman; K.C. Layfield; Katy Gilpatric; Lynne Tobin; Mary Mertz; Monica Goldberg; Nikki Kinkaide; Regina Grund; and Sandy Goldfarb. Ronald Gomez generated marketing ideas.

My father, John Albrecht, bought me my first typewriter. My mother, Virginia Albrecht, inspired me to write. My husband, Ron Klinger, provided technical expertise and partnered with me—as always—every step of the way.

Finally, I want to thank everyone who reads this book and shares its message with friends.

Catherine Klinger ("Dr. K.") wrote the first chapter of this book while living without running water in a log cabin in the mountains of Idaho. At that time, everything she owned fit in a backpack.

Years later—committing to make the workplace more creative and inclusive—the author reentered the mainstream where she climbed Fortune 500 ladders. Her work with CEOs clarified some of the dilemmas examined in this book.

An advocate of spiritual leadership, Dr. K. served as a professor for twenty years. Credentials include a Ph.D. in Organizational Behavior and a Doctorate in Spiritual Studies. She currently lives in Scottsdale where she continues to write.

Change the World

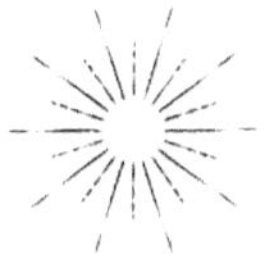

Every 21 seconds a child dies from a water-related disease.

Proceeds from sales are donated to <u>water.org.</u>

Silence Uttered YouTube

(http://youtu.be/P0kyrPkg24s)